UNRAVELING THE TAPESTRY OF ARTIFICIAL INTELLIGENCE: A JOURNEY INTO THE REALM OF INTELLIGENT MACHINES

2

Contents

3

5

Forward

In the reliably creating scene of advancement, one eccentricity has gotten the total imaginative brain and reshaped the restrictions of what we envisioned - Man-made thinking (computerized reasoning). As we stand at the edge of some other time, it ends up being dynamically clear that reenacted insight isn't just a popular articulation anyway a momentous power prepared to change each component of our lives.

Identifying the Covered:

The blend of calculations, information, and computational power that empowers machines to emulate human mental capabilities is at the core of man-made consciousness. From talk affirmation and picture dealing with to autonomous bearing and decisive reasoning, man-made insight hopes to reproduce and work on human information. An embroidery woven with perplexing strings of AI, brain organizations, and profound realizing, all cooperating to make smart frameworks, is uncovered on the excursion into the domain of man-made intelligence.

The Real Odyssey:

The fundamental groundworks of computerized reasoning can be followed back to old legends and old stories, where accounts of automata and vivified objects insinuated the human yearning to revive the inert. In any case, the legitimate commencement of PC based knowledge as a discipline is much of the time credited to the mid-20th hundred years. Leading researchers like Alan Turing envisioned machines that could reproduce any mastered endeavor, laying the reason for the Turing Test - a benchmark for machine information.

The subsequent numerous years saw the volatile development of PC based insight research, put aside by seasons of confidence and defeated assumption. From rule-based ace systems to the approaching of cerebrum associations, the excursion for automated thinking proceeded. Jump advances, for instance, IBM's Dull Blue beating chess grandmaster Garry Kasparov and the climb of normal language dealing with actually look at accomplishments, moving mimicked insight into public awareness.

The Renaissance of simulated intelligence:

The turning point was the resurgence of interest in machine learning, a paradigm in which algorithms learn patterns from data. Another time of computer based intelligence was introduced by the accessibility of broad datasets and progressions in computational capacities. Unexpectedly, machines weren't as of late altered; they were getting the hang of, changing, and progressing.

Brain organizations and profound learning have shown up. Jazzed up by the human psyche, these advanced designs enabled machines to unwind complex models in data, opening excellent capacities. Independent vehicles, picture acknowledgment, and language interpretation all became regular prospects. Computer-based intelligence (CBI) applications quickly spread, reshaping a variety of industries, including manufacturing and entertainment.

Moral Troubles and Social Impacts:

Moral considerations take center stage as the impact of computer-based intelligence spreads throughout society. Requests concerning data security, inclination in computations, and the monetary impact of computerization demand mindful assessment. The ethical compass coordinating the new development and association of mimicked insight becomes pressing as these savvy structures shape our ordinary schedules.

Social repercussions connect past ethics, consolidating money related developments and the inevitable destiny of work. While man-made reasoning ensures capability and headway, it also raises stresses over work evacuating and the prerequisite for deskilling the workforce. For policymakers, organizations, and society as a whole, finding some kind of balance between human prosperity and mechanical advancement has become an essential task.

The New Horizons:

As we cross the convoluted scene of man-made insight, obscure horizons call. Quantum figuring, intelligent man-made reasoning, and interdisciplinary facilitated endeavors hold the responsibility of extra jump advances. The trip into the destiny of PC based knowledge incorporates watching out for challenges, developing inclusivity, and illustrating a course that changes imaginative movement to human characteristics.

In this examination, we leave on a nuanced cognizance of electronic thinking - a story that goes past the computations and code. A journey jumps into the agreeable association among individuals and machines, tending to what reenacted insight can achieve, yet what moral and social frameworks will coordinate its turn of events.

The threads of development, morals, and cultural effect entwine as we unravel the embroidery of man-made reasoning, creating a narrative that rises above the two-dimensional domain of ones and zeros. The journey into the center of recreated knowledge is an odyssey of revelation, introducing hardships and entryways that rename the types of our mechanical future.

1. Distinguish Your Objective:

The most vital phase in any undertaking is to characterize your goal, which provides you an unmistakable guidance for your endeavors. Whether you're leaving on an endeavor, an assessment errand, or encouraging a creative work, an unmistakable objective fills in as a compass to coordinate your exercises and decisions. Coming up next are key thoughts and advances toward help you with portraying your objective effectively:

Make sense of Reason and Expansion:

Recognize the Issue or Opportunity:

Clearly smooth the issue you hope to settle or the entryway you want to utilize. Handle what is happening and the motivation driving your endeavor.

Lay out Unambiguous Goals and Results:

Ensure your objectives are Brilliant (explicit, quantifiable, feasible, applicable, and time-bound). Describe what accomplishment looks like and the outcomes you mean to achieve.

Partners to Consider:

Include significant partners and recognize them. Sort out their perspectives, necessities, and suppositions. This guarantees that your objective aligns with wider interests.

Assessment and Examination:

Direct Field and Statistical surveying:

Research the stream scene associated with your objective. Explore market designs, ferocious scene, or existing game plans. This associates in sorting out the

extraordinary circumstance and anticipated challenges.
SWOT Assessment:

Survey the Characteristics, Weaknesses, Open entryways, and Risks (SWOT) related with your objective. This assessment gives a comprehensive point of view on internal and external factors.

Characterize Significant Measurements:
Assessment of Achievement:

Characterize the key presentation pointers (KPIs) that will be utilized to assess the accomplishment of your objective. These estimations should agree with your goals and results.

Benchmarking:

Choose benchmarks or industry standards relevant to your objective. This helpers in setting sensible suppositions and assessing execution in a greater setting.

Line up with Values and Mission:

Line up with Individual or Progressive Characteristics:

Ensure that your objective lines up with your own characteristics or, in a business setting, with the affiliation's focal objective and values. This plan supports an internal compass and obligation.

Refine and Stress:

Iterative Refinement:

Objectives could create as you collect more information or experience unforeseen hardships. Be accessible to refining and rehashing your objective considering new pieces of information or advancing circumstances.

Set up your objective as a written record:

Make an Unquestionable Attestation:

Arrange your revelations and decisions into an indisputable and reduced statement. This statement should represent the explanation, goals, key estimations, and course of action with values.

Prove Your Objective:

Clearly pass your objective on to significant accomplices. A shared perspective and obligation to the specified goals are guaranteed by this.

By following these methods, you lay out major areas of strength for a point for your endeavor or drive.

Making way for productive preparation, execution, and assessment of your endeavors is the method involved with characterizing your goal.

2. Pick a Structure:

Picking the right system is a vital choice in different fields, from programming improvement to project the board. The development or implementation process is streamlined by a framework's structured approach, tools, and conventions. The following are key contemplations and moves toward assist you with picking a structure successfully:

Figure out Your Necessities:
Distinguish Venture Prerequisites:

Obviously grasp the prerequisites of your undertaking or assignment. Scalability, complexity, and essential functionalities are all important considerations.

Characterize Specialized Limitations:

Know about any specialized imperatives or impediments that might impact your selection of systems. This could incorporate similarity issues, framework prerequisites, or explicit innovation stacks.

Frameworks for available research:

Investigate Existing Structures:

Direct careful exploration on existing structures applicable to your space. Take into consideration

both more recent alternatives and established frameworks.
Local area Backing:

Assess the community of the framework's strength and activity. A powerful local area guarantees progressing backing, refreshes, and an abundance of assets.
Qualitative Documentation:

Evaluate the nature of documentation given by the system. Clear and thorough documentation is fundamental for simplicity of learning and investigating.
Think about Specialized Stack:
Integration with Other Systems:

Guarantee that the picked system is viable with your current innovation stack. This limits coordination challenges and guarantees a smooth improvement process.

Programming Language:

Consider the programming language upheld by the structure. Pick a language that lines up with your group's skill and the undertaking's necessities.
Assess Expectation to absorb information:

Curve of Learning:

Examine the learning curve for each framework. Consider the mastery of your group and the time accessible for preparing.

Engineer Range of abilities:

Assess your group's ongoing range of abilities. Deciding on a system that lines up with your group's skill can speed up the improvement cycle.

Investigate Execution:

Execution Contemplations:

Assess the exhibition benchmarks of every system. Consider factors like speed, asset usage, and versatility, contingent upon your venture's prerequisites.

Security Highlights:

Look at the security highlights given by the structure. Security is central, particularly in applications managing touchy information.

Future Versatility:

Scalability:

Think about the adaptability of the structure. Guarantee that the picked structure can develop with your task and oblige expanded request.

Seller Lock-in:

Survey the level of merchant secure related with the structure. Choose structures that give adaptability and limit conditions on a particular seller.

Settle on an Educated Choice:
Model and Test:

Utilizing various frameworks, create prototypes or small experiments if possible. This active methodology can uncover experiences into usability and reasonableness.

Collect input from stakeholders:

Accumulate input from pertinent partners, including engineers, project chiefs, and end-clients. Their points of view can furnish significant bits of knowledge and guarantee arrangement with project objectives.

Archive Your Choice:

Make a Choice Network:

Report your assessment models and the scores allotted to every structure. A choice grid can give an organized outline and work with an information driven dynamic cycle.

Make your decision known:

Obviously convey the picked system to all partners. Guarantee that everybody in question knows about the choice reasoning and the advantages it brings to the task.

By following these means, you can go with an educated choice while choosing a system, making way for a fruitful and proficient turn of events or execution process.

3. Collect Data:

Gathering information is a basic move toward different spaces, going from logical exploration to business examination. The quality and importance of the information you gather altogether influence the results of your venture. Here are key contemplations and moves toward assist you with social occasion information successfully:

Characterize Information Necessities:

Distinguish Information Goals:

Define your data collection's goals in detail. Know what specific information or insights you want to get from the data.

Indicate Information Types:

Distinguish the sorts of information expected for your task. This could incorporate quantitative information (numbers, estimations) or subjective information (depictions, perceptions).

Plan Your Information Assortment:

Foster an Information Assortment Plan:

Make an organized arrangement framing how you will gather information. Characterize the procedures, instruments, and assets required.

Think about Moral and Legitimate Contemplations:

Be aware of moral contemplations and lawful necessities connected with information assortment. Guarantee that your techniques consent to security guidelines and moral principles.

Pick Information Sources:

Choose Your Primary Sources:

Find the primary sources of your data. This could include gathering information straightforwardly from people, sensors, or other firsthand techniques.

Investigate Optional Sources:

Explore existing datasets or optional sources that might be applicable to your undertaking. This could be data that is available to the public, reports from the industry, or academic studies.

Plan Information Assortment Strategies:

Select Information Assortment Strategies:

Pick suitable techniques for social affair information in view of your goals. Surveys, interviews, observations, experiments, and data scraping are all common methods.

Foster Review or Survey:

If pertinent, plan a review or poll that lines up with your examination objectives. Guarantee that questions are clear, impartial, and applicable to your goals.

Pilot Testing:

Organize Pilot Tests:

Before full-scale information assortment, direct pilot tests to recognize and resolve any issues with your information assortment strategies. This guarantees the unwavering quality and legitimacy of your information.

Lay out Information Quality Control:

Carry out Quality Control Measures:

Set up measures to control and keep up with information quality. This incorporates information cleaning, approval checks, and tending to exceptions or irregularities.

Guarantee Consistency:

Normalize information assortment strategies to guarantee consistency across various sources and time spans. Consistency is urgent for significant investigation.

Think about Examining:

Characterize Inspecting Procedure:

Define a sampling strategy if working with a large population is impractical. This includes choosing a delegate subset of the populace for information assortment.

Randomization:

Include randomization in your sampling procedure, if necessary. Irregular examples improve the generalizability of your discoveries.

Information Capacity and Security:

Lay out Information Stockpiling Convention:

Decide how and where you will store the gathered information. Consider safety efforts to safeguard delicate data.

Information Encryption:

If managing delicate information, carry out encryption conventions to shield data during capacity and transmission.

Train Information Gatherers:

Train Information Authorities:

In the event that numerous people are associated with information assortment, give preparing to guarantee consistency in the utilization of information assortment strategies.

Record the Cycle:

Report Information Assortment Methods:

Obviously report the strategies followed during information assortment. This documentation is significant for straightforwardness and replicability.

Audit and Emphasize:

Ceaseless Survey:

Persistently survey the information assortment process. If necessary, make changes or refinements in light of criticism or arising experiences.

Emphasize if Essential:

Prepare to iterate on your data collection strategy in the event that initial data collection yields unexpected findings or difficulties. Adaptability is vital to adjusting to evolving conditions.

You will be able to effectively collect data if you follow these steps. Whether directing exploration, market investigation, or any information driven project, a professional information assortment process improves the dependability and legitimacy of your discoveries.

4. Preprocess Information:

Information preprocessing is a urgent move toward the

information examination pipeline that includes cleaning, putting together, and changing crude information into a configuration reasonable for additional investigation or model preparation. Here are key contemplations and moves toward guide you through the information preprocessing stage:

Initial Analysis of the Data:
Know the characteristics of the data:

Understanding the nature of your data is the first step. Distinguish information types, organizations, and likely issues. This incorporates perceiving missing qualities, anomalies, and any examples that might impact preprocessing choices.

Handle Missing Information:

Imputing values or removing incomplete records can be used to address missing data. The decision is based on how much information is missing and how it will affect your analysis.

Cleaning the Data:

Eliminate Copies:

Distinguish and eliminate copy records to guarantee information honesty. Copies might twist investigation results and lead to one-sided ends.

Handle Exceptions:

Assess and deal with anomalies appropriately. Outliers may be kept, corrected, or removed with proper documentation, depending on the context.

Information Change:

Normalize or Standardize:

Normalize or standardize mathematical highlights to guarantee they are on a reliable scale. This is especially significant for AI calculations delicate to the extent of factors.

Encode Absolute Factors:

Convert clear cut factors into a mathematical configuration utilizing methods like one-hot encoding or name encoding. This works with the consideration of clear cut information in AI models.

Include Designing:

Make new elements that could improve the prescient force of your model. This could include numerical changes, consolidating existing elements, or separating pertinent data.

Time Series Information Contemplations:

Handle Time-Related Elements:

Time-related features should be handled appropriately if your data contains time series. This could incorporate resembling, slacking, or separating fleeting highlights.

Data Processing for Text:

Text Tokenization and Factorization:

If managing text information, tokenize and vectorize the text into mathematical organization. Methods, for example, TF-IDF or word embeddings can be utilized.

Eliminate Stop words and Exceptional Characters:

Take out insignificant words (stopwords) and extraordinary characters from message information to zero in on fundamental data.

Information Reconciliation:

Consolidation or Join Datasets:

On the off chance that your examination includes different datasets, union or go along with them properly. Guarantee that the consolidating system lines up with your examination objectives.

Dealing with Imbalanced Information:

Take Care of Uneven Classes:

On the off chance that managing imbalanced classes in characterization issues, utilize strategies, for example, oversampling, under sampling, or utilizing manufactured information to adjust class appropriation.

Reduction of Dimensionality and Scaling:

Apply Dimensionality Decrease:

Use strategies like Head Part Examination (PCA) to lessen the dimensionality of the dataset, particularly if managing high-layered information.

Scale Highlights:

Scale mathematical highlights to bring them inside a comparable reach, particularly if utilizing calculations delicate to include scales.

Information Parting:

Divide the data into two sets, one for testing

Partition your dataset into preparing and testing sets. This guarantees that your model is

assessed on information it has not seen during preparing.
Reporting and Forming:
Archive Preprocessing Steps:

Keep up with itemized documentation of all preprocessing steps applied to the information. This documentation is pivotal for straightforwardness, replication, and investigating.
Version Management:

Set up version control for your preprocessing scripts and datasets. This helps track changes and guarantees reproducibility.
Audit and Emphasize:
Ceaseless Survey:
Persistently audit the effect of preprocessing on your examination or model execution. Be ready to

emphasize in view of experiences acquired during examination.

By perseveringly preprocessing your information, you improve the quality and dependability of resulting investigations or AI models. This stage is urgent for revealing significant examples and experiences inside your information.

5. Pick Model Design:

Picking the right model design is a critical choice in creating AI or profound learning frameworks. The engineering decides how your model will handle data, learn examples, and make expectations. Here are key contemplations and moves toward guide you through the method involved with picking a model engineering:

Characterize the Issue and Targets:

Comprehend the Issue Type:

Decide if your concern is a grouping, relapse, bunching, or another sort. The idea of the issue will impact the decision of model engineering.

Set Execution Measurements:

Characterize the measurements that will be utilized to assess the exhibition of your model. These measurements rely upon the idea of your concern (exactness, accuracy, review, F1 score, and so forth.).

Investigate Existing Designs:

Audit Existing Models:

Look into existing models that have worked well for similar jobs. This could incorporate notable

structures, for example, convolutional brain organizations (CNNs) for picture handling or intermittent brain organizations (RNNs) for successive information.
Move Learning:

Consider utilizing pre-prepared models and move learning, particularly if your dataset isn't broad. This can boost performance on other tasks by utilizing knowledge gained from one.

Think about the Size of Your Dataset:

Size of Dataset:

The size of your dataset can impact your decision of model engineering. Profound brain networks frequently require huge datasets to sum up well. In the event that your dataset is little, consider less difficult models or structures intended for move learning.

Interpretability versus complexity:

Model Intricacy:

Examine the trade-off between model interpretability and complexity. Deep neural networks and other more complex models, like them, may provide superior performance but may be more challenging to comprehend.

Interpretability Necessities:

Consider whether interpretability is pivotal for your application. Assuming this is the case, less difficult models like choice trees or straight models might be liked.

Tending to Over fitting:

Regularization Strategies:

Pick designs that incorporate regularization procedures to forestall overfitting. Strategies like dropout, L1 or L2 regularization, and early halting can be useful.

Models for Explicit Information Types:

Based on the data type, choose an architecture:

Various kinds of information (pictures, text, time series) frequently require explicit designs. For instance, Convolution Brain Organizations (CNNs) are appropriate for picture information, while Repetitive Brain Organizations (RNNs) are intended for successive information.

Hyper parameter Tuning:

Hyper parameter Tuning:

Calibrate hyper parameters for your picked engineering. This incorporates learning rates, clump sizes, and different boundaries well defined for the picked model.

Assess Computational Assets:

Think about Computational Assets: Survey the computational assets accessible. Deep neural network models, in particular, can be computationally expensive. Choose a model that works with the resources you have.

Approval and Testing:

Perform Cross-Approval:

Utilize cross-approval to survey how well your picked engineering sums up to various subsets of the information.

Assess on Test Set:

Assess your model on a different test set that it hasn't seen during preparing or approval. This gives a practical gauge of its exhibition on new, concealed information.

Archive Your Choice:

Make a Model Engineering Record:

Record the picked model engineering, including the reasoning behind the choice, hyper parameters, and a particular contemplations.

Audit and Emphasize:

Ceaseless Survey:

Ceaselessly survey the presentation of your model in certifiable situations. Be ready to emphasize on the design if necessary in view of execution and criticism.

Via cautiously considering these elements and steps, you can pick a model design that lines up with the necessities of your undertaking, information, and accessible assets. Recall that the decision of design is definitely not a one-size-fits-all choice and ought to be custom-made to the particulars of your concern and goals.

6. Assemble and Prepare Model:

Building and preparing an AI model includes executing the picked model engineering, taking care of it with your arranged dataset, and changing its boundaries to gain designs from the information. Here are key contemplations and moves toward guide you through the most common way of building and preparing your model:

Arrangement Climate:
Introduce Fundamental Libraries:

Ensure you have the necessary libraries and conditions introduced. Normal libraries incorporate TensorFlow, PyTorch, scikit-learn, or others relying upon the picked structure.

Climate Arrangement:

Set up your improvement climate, including virtual conditions if necessary, to oversee conditions and guarantee reproducibility.

Put the Model Architecture into Action:

Architecture of a Code Model:

Carry out the picked model engineering utilizing the programming language and profound learning system of your decision. This includes characterizing layers, actuation capabilities, and any custom parts.

Actually take a look at Model Synopsis:

Print or envision a rundown of your model engineering to confirm that it matches your assumptions and to check for any startling issues.

Plan Information for Preparing:

Information Pipeline:

Foster an information input pipeline to take care of your information into the model during preparing productively. This might incorporate clustering, rearranging, and preprocessing steps.

Divide Information:

In the event that not done during preprocessing, split your dataset into preparing, approval, and testing sets. The preparation set is utilized to prepare the model, the approval set helps tune hyperparameters, and the test set assesses last execution.

Design Preparing Boundaries:

Characterize Misfortune Capability:

Pick a proper misfortune capability in light of your concern type (e.g., mean squared blunder for relapse, cross-entropy for arrangement).
Select Analyzer:

Pick an enhancer (e.g., Adam, SGD) to limit the misfortune capability during preparing. Change the learning rate in light of the attributes of your concern and model.
Measurements for Assessment:

Characterize assessment measurements (e.g., exactness, accuracy, review) to screen the exhibition of your model during preparing and approval.

Train the Model:

Introduce Loads:

Make the model's weights initial. For the model to begin learning effectively, this step is essential.

Preparing Circle:

Execute the preparation circle, which includes emphasizing through your preparation information, forward-going it through the model, ascertaining the misfortune, and backpropagating to refresh loads.

Approval Circle:

Intermittently assess your model on the approval set during preparing to screen its exhibition and identify overfitting.

Change Hyperparameters:

Adjust hyperparameters in light of the presentation saw during preparing and approval. This might include changing learning rates, bunch sizes, or different boundaries.

Visualize and monitor training:

Keep track of training progress:

Use apparatuses like TensorBoard or custom logging to screen key measurements and envision preparing progress.

Picture Model Results:

To ensure that model outputs meet expectations, visualize them on sample data. This can assist with recognizing issues from the get-go in the preparation cycle.

Save Model:

Save Model Designated spots:

Save designated spots of your model during preparing to continue preparing from a particular point or utilize the prepared model for surmising later.

Assess on Test Set:

Last Assessment:

Assess your prepared model on the test set to evaluate its exhibition on inconspicuous information. This gives a sensible proportion of how well the model sums up.

Report Model Preparation:

Make Preparing Report:

Record key subtleties of the preparation interaction, including hyper parameters, execution measurements, and any difficulties confronted. This documentation helps with reproducibility and investigating.

Audit and Emphasize:

Ceaseless Survey:

Consistently audit the model's presentation and be ready to repeat on the preparation interaction. Changing hyper parameters, acquiring more data, or improving the model's architecture are all examples of this.
Model Tweaking:

On the off chance that the model doesn't meet wanted execution, consider adjusting its engineering, gathering extra information, or exploring different avenues regarding progressed preparing strategies.
By following these means, you can successfully construct and train an AI model. Keep in mind that model training is an iterative process in which domain expertise, high-quality data, and fine-tuning model

parameters are often the keys to success.

7. Assess Model:

Assessing an AI model is a critical stage to guarantee its viability, speculation, and arrangement with project goals. Here are key contemplations and moves toward guide you through the method involved with assessing your model:

Characterize Assessment Measurements:

Select Significant Measurements:

Pick assessment measurements that line up with the goals of your task. Normal measurements incorporate exactness, accuracy, review, F1 score for grouping, and mean squared blunder for relapse.

Space Explicit Measurements:

If necessary, think about metrics specific to the domain. Sensitivity and specificity, for instance, might be more important than overall accuracy in medical applications.
Assess on Test Set:
Test Set Execution:

Assess your model on the test set, which comprises of information not seen during preparing or approval. This gives a fair-minded evaluation of how well your model sums up to new, inconspicuous information.
Disarray Network:

For grouping issues, make a disarray grid to figure out the conveyance of genuine up-sides, genuine negatives, bogus up-sides, and misleading negatives.

ROC Bend and AUC:

If managing double order, examine the Collector Working Trademark (ROC) bend and ascertain the Region Under the Bend (AUC) to survey the model's capacity to recognize classes.

Cross-Validation:

Cross-Validation:

If relevant, perform cross-approval to survey the model's exhibition across various subsets of the information. This gives a more hearty assessment by averaging results over numerous folds.

Interpretability:

Model Interpretability:

Evaluate the interpretability of your model. Contingent upon your application, understanding how the model settles on choices might be urgent.

Feature's Relevance:

Dissect include significance to comprehend which information highlights contribute most to the model's expectations. This is especially important for model explain ability and decision-making.

Tending to Predisposition:

Assess Predisposition:

Look for bias in the model, especially if it includes sensitive characteristics like race, gender, or age. To ensure that the results of the model are ethical and fair, employ methods that can identify and reduce bias.

Contrast and Gauge:

Comparative Evaluation:

Compare the performance of your model to that of a baseline model or a straightforward rule-based approach. This decides whether your model gives significant upgrades over a fundamental arrangement.

Vigor and Speculation:

Vigor Testing:

Assess the model's power by testing it on information that could vary from the preparation dispersion. This could incorporate uproarious information, exceptions, or information from an alternate source.

Speculation to New Information:

Introduce new data or simulate situations that were not in the training set to test the model's generalization.

Model Dependableness:

Logic Strategies:

In the event that material, utilize model reasonableness methods to grasp the thinking behind unambiguous forecasts. For applications where interpretability is crucial, this is essential.

Archive Assessment Results:

Make a report on the evaluation:

Report the aftereffects of your model assessment, including measurements, representations, and any noticed difficulties. The dissemination of findings to stakeholders requires this documentation.

Improve and Iterate:

Continuous Improvement:

Iterate on the model if its performance falls short of expectations. This could include returning to the preprocessing steps, changing hyper parameters,

or exploring different avenues regarding various models.
Loop Feedback:

Lay out a criticism circle for persistent improvement. Assemble criticism from clients or partners and use it to refine your model over the long haul.
Consider Business Effect:
Business Effect Evaluation:
Evaluate the effect of your model on business targets. Comprehend how the model's forecasts convert into significant experiences and upgrades.
Convey or Repeat:
Choice to Convey or Repeat:

In view of the assessment results and criticism, conclude whether the model is prepared for arrangement

or on the other hand in the event that further cycles are vital.
Convey and Screen:

In the case of conveying the model, execute checking components to follow its presentation in certifiable situations. This helps identify any performance degradation and ensures ongoing dependability.
By following these means, you can methodically assess your AI model, guaranteeing that it meets the ideal measures and is strategically set up to add to your undertaking's targets. Model evaluation is an ongoing process, and long-term success necessitates constant improvement and monitoring.

8. Fine-Tune:

Calibrating an AI model includes making gradual changes in

accordance with further develop its exhibition in view of assessment results and criticism. This iterative cycle is fundamental for advancing the model for true situations. Here are key contemplations and moves toward guide you through the tweaking stage:

Break down Assessment Results:
Audit Assessment Measurements:

Return to the assessment measurements and results got during the model assessment stage. Recognize regions where the model performed well and regions that need improvement.
Decipher Misclassifications:

Investigate misclassifications or blunders made by the model. Comprehend the examples or sorts of information guides that the model battles toward handle.

Hyperparameter Tuning:

Change Hyperparameters:

Adjust hyperparameters like dropout rates, regularization strengths, and learning rates. Little changes can essentially influence model execution.

Network Search or Irregular Hunt:

Use network search or irregular pursuit methods to efficiently investigate a scope of hyperparameter values. This distinguishes ideal setups all the more productively.

Model Engineering Changes:

Alter Design:

Consider making changes to the model engineering in light of bits of

knowledge acquired from assessment. This could include adding or eliminating layers, changing actuation works, or integrating extra elements.
Ensemble Approaches:

Investigate ensemble methods by combining a number of models to make use of the strengths of each one. This can upgrade in general execution and heartiness.

Information Expansion:
Apply Information Expansion:
Use data augmentation strategies, if necessary, to artificially diversify your training dataset. This assists the model with summing up better to concealed varieties in the information.

Regularization Strategies:
Adjust Regularization:

Change regularization procedures to forestall overfitting. Explore different avenues regarding various qualities of regularization, dropout rates, or different methods to track down the right equilibrium.

Move Learning:

Further Use Move Learning:

In the case of utilizing move learning, try different things with various pre-prepared models or calibrate more or less layers. This permits you to adjust the pre-prepared information to your particular errand.

Tending to Predisposition and Reasonableness:

Alleviate Predisposition:

Assuming predisposition is distinguished in the model forecasts, carry out methods to relieve predisposition. This could include re-inspecting procedures, changing class loads, or utilizing decency mindful calculations.

Iterative Model Preparation:

Training by Iteration:

Perform model training, evaluation, and fine-tuning in multiple rounds. Every cycle carries the model nearer to ideal execution.

Cross-Validation:

Cross-Approval Reassessment:

In the case of utilizing cross-approval, reconsider your model's exhibition after each tweaking emphasis. This guarantees that upgrades sum up across various subsets of the information.

Screen Approval Execution:

Screen Approval Execution:

Ceaselessly screen the model's presentation on the approval set during the calibrating system. This forestalls overfitting and guarantees upgrades mean speculation.

Documentation:

Update Documentation:

Stay up with the latest with subtleties of the adjusting system. Report changes made, purposes for changes, and any examples got the hang of during the iterative refinement.

Joint effort and Input:

Work together with Partners:

Team up with partners, space specialists, and end-clients to accumulate criticism. Their experiences can give important points of view on model execution and possible enhancements.

Choosing Point:

Check if you're ready to be deployed:

Make regular checks to see if the model is ready for use. Think about elements like in general execution, soundness, and arrangement with business targets.

Convey or Calibrate:

Choose whether to send the model in a certifiable setting or tweak. The urgency of deployment, business requirements, and model performance at the moment may all influence the decision.

Consistent Improvement:

Lay out Persistent Improvement Cycles:

Even after deployment, implement processes for continuous improvement. Consistently screen model execution, assemble client criticism, and emphasize in light of advancing necessities.

By methodically calibrating your model, you can improve its capacities and address explicit difficulties experienced during the assessment stage. The tweaking system is a fundamental part of fostering an AI arrangement that conveys significant and solid outcomes in different genuine situations.

9. Create Result:

Producing yield with regards to an AI project regularly alludes to utilizing the prepared model to make expectations on new, inconspicuous information. Here are the vital contemplations and steps engaged with producing yield from your AI model:

Input Information Readiness:
Preprocess New Information:

If you have new, concealed information, preprocess it utilizing similar advances applied to the preparation information. Guarantee consistency in preprocessing moves toward keep up with the model's assumptions.
Highlight Scaling and Encoding:

Apply a similar element scaling and encoding changes utilized during preparing to guarantee the information's similarity with the model.
Model Deduction:
Utilize Prepared Model:

After you have evaluated and fine-tuned the trained model, load it. Guarantee the model is in a similar state as when it created the best outcomes during assessment.

Prediction of a Batch:

For proficiency, perform cluster expectations assuming managing numerous relevant pieces of information. This is especially significant while conveying models in genuine applications.

Post-Processing:

Steps After Processing:

Apply any necessary post-processing steps to the predictions generated by the model. This could incorporate changing over likelihood scores to class names or planning mathematical forecasts to significant results.

Interpretation:

Decipher Model Forecasts:

Comprehend and decipher the model forecasts with regards to your concern. Think about what the model's outputs mean and how they can help you make decisions.

Visualizations:

Imagine Expectations:

Make perceptions or reports to successfully impart the model forecasts. This is particularly significant in applications where partners need to comprehend and follow up on the model's experiences.

Deployment:

Send the Model:

On the off chance that the model is sent in a creation climate, coordinate it into your application or framework. Make sure it seamlessly integrates with the workflow and can handle predictions in real time or in batches as needed.

Screen Model Execution:

Observing Framework:

Set up a monitoring system to keep an eye on how the model does in the environment where it is being used. Screen measurements like exactness, accuracy, and review, and be aware of any float in the information circulation.

UI:

UI Joining:

If relevant, coordinate the model forecasts into a UI or application. This guarantees that end-clients can without much of a stretch access and decipher the model's results.

Blunder Taking care of:

Blunder Dealing with Components:

Carry out hearty blunder dealing with systems in the organization climate. Address any unforeseen issues quickly to keep up with the unwavering quality of the model in true situations.

Documentation:

Update Documentation:

Update documentation to incorporate insights concerning the sent model, including input prerequisites, yield translation, and any contemplations for clients.

Consistent Improvement:

Loop Feedback:

Lay out a criticism circle to assemble bits of knowledge from the sent model's exhibition. Utilize this input to illuminate future emphasess, enhancements, and updates.

Cooperation and Correspondence:

Partner Correspondence:

Convey the model results really to partners. Give clarifications or representations that assist clients with figuring out the thinking behind the model's expectations.

Ethical and compliance considerations:

Consistence and Morals:

Guarantee consistence with important guidelines and moral contemplations, particularly while conveying models in delicate spaces. Address issues connected with inclination, reasonableness, and protection.

Create Reports or Results:

Create Reports:

In the event that your model produces reports or outlines, create these results in light of the information. Reports could incorporate bits of knowledge, suggestions, or some other pertinent data.

Continuous Improvement:

Permanent Iteration:

Constantly emphasize on the sent model in light of execution criticism, evolving prerequisites, or developing information disseminations. Updates can be applied as needed to keep or improve the effectiveness of the model.

You can effectively generate output from your machine learning model in a development or production environment by following these steps. The most important thing is to make certain that the predictions made by the model are in line with the goals that were intended and provide useful information for making decisions.

10. Send (Discretionary):

Sending of an AI model includes making the model accessible for use in a creation climate, permitting it to produce expectations on new, concealed information. Here are key contemplations and moves toward guide you through the arrangement cycle:

Setup of the Infrastructure:
Select Sending Stage:

Based on the needs you have for your infrastructure, select a deployment platform. Depending on the application, options include cloud services (AWS, Azure, Google Cloud), on-premises servers, or edge devices.
Foundation Provisioning:

Arrangement the vital framework to host and serve your model. Configuring resources in the cloud, containers, or servers are all examples of this.
Model Serialization:
Model Serializing:

Create a serial file of your trained model that is compatible with the deployment environment you have chosen. TensorFlow SavedModel, ONNX, or serialized versions specific to the framework are all common formats.

Model Serving:

Launch the Model Server:

Set up a model serving climate. This could include sending a committed model serving server, using serverless capabilities, or coordinating with model serving stages like TensorFlow Serving or TensorFlow Light for edge gadgets.

Programming interface Improvement:

Programming interface Improvement:

Foster a Programming interface (Application Programming Point of interaction) to uncover your model for expectations. Characterize information and result configurations, and carry out endpoints to get new information and return model forecasts.

Endpoint Design:

Design Endpoint:

Set the URL or address where clients can send predictions requests to the deployment endpoint.

Considerations for Scaling:

Strategy for Scaling:

Plan for adaptability by thinking about the normal responsibility. Carry out techniques for scaling evenly or in an upward direction in light of interest.

Safety efforts:

Put security measures into action:

Protect the API and deployed model with security measures. Use confirmation systems, encryption, and other security practices to guarantee information trustworthiness and classification.

Monitoring:

Checking and Logging:

Set up checking and logging instruments to follow the presentation of your conveyed model. Screen key measurements, for example, reaction time, blunder rates, and asset utilization.

Version Management:

Model Forming:

Execute variant control for your sent model. You can manage updates, rollbacks, and A/B testing of various model versions with this.

Documentation:

Programming interface Documentation:

Record the Programming interface and arrangement process. Give clear directions on how clients or applications can associate with the sent model through the Programming interface.

Testing:

Joining Testing:

Make sure that the deployed model works as expected in the production environment by running extensive integration tests. Confirm that information input/yield, reaction times, and mistake dealing with meet necessities.

A/B testing is an option:

A/B Testing:

Consider executing A/B testing to look at the presentation of numerous model forms or setups in a live climate. This helps settle on informed conclusions about model updates.

Constant Arrangement (Discretionary):

Nonstop Sending Pipeline:

On the off chance that doable, set up a nonstop sending pipeline that mechanizes the sending system at whatever point there are updates to the model or its conditions.

Consistence and Administration:

Consistence and Administration:

Guarantee consistence with guidelines and administration arrangements pertinent to your application. Address issues connected with information protection, security, and moral contemplations.

Rollback Plan:

Rollback Plan:

Have a rollback plan set up in the event that issues emerge after sending. Reverting to a stable previous model version or configuration is what this entails.

Communication with Users:

Speak with Clients:

Assuming that the sending influences end-clients or partners, impart the changes, benefits, and any fundamental guidelines. Offer help channels for tending to client questions or issues.

Improve and Iterate:

Consistent Improvement:

Based on observing feedback, user experience, and shifting requirements, develop procedures for ongoing improvement. Emphasize on the conveyed model to improve its presentation after some time.

Execution Streamlining:

Streamline Execution:

Constantly improve the exhibition of your sent model. This could include adjusting designs, tending to bottlenecks, or enhancing surmising speed.

Consistence Approval:

Approval Checks:

Approve that the conveyed model consents to administrative necessities and inner arrangements. This might include ordinary reviews and checks to guarantee progressing consistence.

Sending is a basic stage that changes your AI model from an improvement climate to a true application. Cautious preparation, exhaustive testing, and constant checking are fundamental to guarantee the dependability, security, and execution of the conveyed model.

End

With everything taken into account, the most widely recognized approach to making and conveying a computer based intelligence model is an intricate trip that incorporates careful readiness, intentional execution, and unending refinement. Each stage, from describing objectives to show sending, expects a crucial part in the advancement of the general undertaking. Here are key central focuses:

Clear Targets are Focal:

Portray your objectives clearly before leaving on the man-made intelligence adventure. Understand the issue you are endeavoring to handle, the sort of data open, and the best outcomes.
Need is given to information quality:

First class data is the supporting of productive artificial intelligence projects. To guarantee the unwavering quality of your model,

devote time and effort to information gathering, preprocessing, and approval.
The Choice of a Model Design Requires Care:

Picking a reasonable model plan incorporates considering the possibility of your data, issue type, and open resources. In view of the consequences of the assessment, consistently survey and emphasize over the model design.
Effective Arrangement and Appraisal are Iterative:

Iterative cycles are utilized in the periods of preparing and assessment. Align hyperparameters, change the model designing, and rehash considering evaluation results to achieve ideal execution.

Conscientious organization is required:

Sending a model incorporates considerations like establishment plan, Programming point of interaction improvement, security, and noticing. For a smooth change from improvement to creation, give close consideration to these viewpoints.

Steady Improvement is Basic:

Computer based intelligence models are not static; they should be continually dealt with considering analysis, creating requirements, and changing data transports. Spread out processes for unending checking, accentuation, and improvement.

Think about Moral and Consistence Points of view:

All through the entire man-made intelligence lifecycle, ponder moral repercussions and consistence with rules. Address tendency, fairness, assurance, and security stresses to ensure trustworthy and moral PC based knowledge improvement.
Correspondence and Documentation Matter:

It is fundamental to discuss really with partners, clients, and colleagues. Report your cycles, decisions, and model nuances totally to work with collaboration, straightforwardness, and reproducibility.
Have a go at Interpretability:

Where possible, go all in. Fathom and convey how your model chooses, especially in applications where interpretability is crucial for client trust and understanding.

Find a balance between complexity and simplicity:

Find the right concordance between model unpredictability and ease. Complex models could offer world class execution anyway can be all the more sincerely to translate and stay aware of. Think about the trade offs considering the specific prerequisites of your endeavor.

You will have a better chance of developing and distributing an AI model that not only meets your goals but also makes a significant contribution to your organization and the wider community as a whole if you adhere to these guidelines and employ a comprehensive approach. Recollect that simulated intelligence is a novel field, and staying educated about new turns regarding occasions and best practices is principal for continued with progress.